X/4

9/99 540

1/02

W9-CFI-737

A Small Thing Like A Breath

Poetry by
Anthony Abbott

To the memory of
my daughter

CAROLYN DEAN ABBOTT
(1963-1967)

ACKNOWLEDGMENTS

South Coast Poetry Review: "My Dog, The Lover"
St. Andrews Review: "Far From Home"
Southern Poetry Review: "The Beginning"
Crucible: "The Poet, The Lovers, and The Nuns,"
            "Longings," "Poem for Anne", "News Story",
            "Words Are the Only Fingers"
Lyricist: "Lost and Found," "Words," "Stirring the
            Muse," "Lines Composed...," "The Girl
            Speaks of the Carousel," "Stone Soup",
            "Another Kind of Secret"
Anglican Theological Review: "Jesus Saves"
Lullwater Review: "The Muse Is Angry," "The Muse Is
            Sullen," "The Muse Is Silent," "The Muse
            Has Gone","The Legendary Stillness of Herons"
Oxalis: "Twenty-Twenty", "Ian Donald"
Sanskrit: "Apple Blossoms"
Tar River Poetry: "Dust Beneath My Shoe"
The Arts Journal: "Le Mont St. Michel," "Vezelay"
Synaethesia: "On Seeing St. Joan Once Again"
Pembroke: "Remembrance", "Carrot Colored Words"
G. W. Review: "Ely Cathedral: Toward Evensong"
Theology Today: "Chartres Revisited: To A Critic," "Santa
            Camisia"
Charlotte Poetry Review: "The Mole Flower," "Silence"
Wellspring: "The Dancer Speaks to Her Ex-Lover"
Mt. Olive Review: "Night Crazies"

ISBN: 1-879934-16-7

Printed by: PBM Graphics
               Durham, North Carolina
For: St. Andrews Press
               Laurinburg, North Carolina

This book made possible through the
Richard Walser and
Bernice Kelley Harris Fund
of the St. Andrews Press

Contents

I. A SMALL THING LIKE A BREATH

A Small Thing Like A Breath   1
On The Terror of Being Chosen Last   3
    in Kickball
Growing Up   5
Time of Day   7
Ian Donald   8
The Boy, Seventeen Visits His Mother   9
    in the Hospital
Of Catchers   11
Sandwiches   12
My Dog, The Lover   13
Walking the Dog   14
College Days   16
Sacre Coeur: Christmas Eve   17
Lines Composed   19
The Dancer Speaks To Her Ex-Lover   21
News Story   23

II. FAR FROM HOME

Far From Home   26
Jesus Saves   28
Christmas Vespers   30
Longings   31
The Poet, The Lovers and the Nuns   32
Le Mont St. Michel   35
Vezelay   36
Chartres Revisited: To A Critic   38
Sancta Camisia   40
Ely Cathedral: Toward Evensong   41
On Seeing St. Joan Once Again   43
Hurricane   44
The Girl Speaks of the Carousel   45
My Good Angel   46

III. LOST AND FOUND

Lost and Found   50
The Soul Waits Under The Door of   52
     Silence
Stirring the Muse   53
The Muse Is Angry   55
The Muse Is Sullen   56
The Muse Is Silent   57
The Muse Is Gone   58
Silence   59
Words   60
Stone Soup   61
Another Kind of Secret   62
Words Are The Only Fingers   63

IV. THE MOLE FLOWER

The Mole Flower   68
The Beginning   70
On the Second Day   71
Dust Beneath My Shoe   72
Remembrance   73
Apple Blossoms   75
Night Crazies   76
Poem for Anne   80
Turtle   81
Carrot Colored Words   84
The Legendary Stillness of Herons   86
Thousand Petalled Lotus   90

A SMALL THING LIKE A BREATH

A SMALL THING LIKE A BREATH
For James and Robert

How cheap words are. How easy to say,
"I love you," knowing not even the surface
of the word. How easy to say, "I'd die for you,"
knowing not even the icy edge of death, not even
his outer garments.

Then you bear a child. You carry a life
in the darkness of your womb for nine uneasy
months. The child descends, bumping the fragile
edges of its unformed skull against the walls
of your pelvic bone. He enters the world wailing.

For a time the machines help him breathe.
You cannot hold him because of the wires,
the sensors which monitor each vital function
and so you sit by his side and give him your
finger to hold, and you watch his tiny,
perfectly formed nails curl around you
and after many hours you are still not tired,
not finished marveling at the wonder you have
created and you know that you could, indeed
would die for this son, this glorious, heartbreaking,
selfish, beautiful son.

And every night you continue
to marvel, week after week, month after month.
Every night before sleep you tiptoe into his room
and listen to each small breath and watch the way
he seems to smile and how his eyelashes curl upward.
And later you will keep pictures, you will mark
his first step and the awkward, rounded shapes
of his first letters. You will shout with joy
for his first line drive and cry for the pink
cotton sheep he makes in Sunday school on Easter.

And when he hurts you will know the very marrow
of love, how pain for his pain takes you
in its arms and grips like icy night. Then,
when you speak of love and death, you will do so
not lightly, but with bowed head and hushed respect
for a small thing like a breath.

ON THE TERROR OF BEING CHOSEN LAST IN KICKBALL

The playground is bad enough
just being there
standing outside at recess
pushed through the door by Coach Roberts
with his fat muscles and his teeth.
"It's good for you," he laughs.
Good for who?" I think with the sun
so bright it makes me squint
and the other guys talking, smiling
showing the purple notes they got from girls.

The playground is bad enough.
But then the voice of Billy or Paul
comes bouncing to my ears,
LET'S PLAY KICKBALL.

Worse than bats inside your bed
worse than mothers kissing you
in front of all your friends.
LET'S PLAY KICKBALL.

And everyone runs, actually RUNS
to where the game will start
waving their silly hands like daffodills.
"Pick me, pick me," they say
"Pick me, pick me, I'll play all day."

And then they turn their heads and see—
ME. You laugh. You think it's funny
but that's because when you were small
you never kicked the ball straight up
into your own nose, making your glasses fall
into the yellow dust beside home plate.

You were never chosen last
after the Chinese kid who couldn't even talk
after the boy who wore his pants so high
his belly button showed when he unzipped his fly.
Even after all the girls
who even if they couldn't kick
would giggle like little sticks
shaking in the wind telling the boys
they couldn't throw them out above the waist.

Because you never swung and missed
and landed on your seat, your hat
descending down your face
to magnify your team's disgrace
you were never chosen last.

GROWING UP

Why do they call it up? Why not growing <u>out</u>?
or older or colder, but certainly not bolder.
If <u>up</u> is the long mouthed faces who drive
their barred cars to work down the choking asphalt
roads, then I'm for <u>down</u> or even <u>back</u>.

You know the grown up guy in the ad who's eating
frosted flakes with Tony the Tiger chuckling
over his shoulder? Well, that's me. Why not?

What's so hot about up? Where's the Lorax
in up? Where's Jiminy Cricket wishing on a star
in the forest where the wild things are?

My world is a tea-party. No, not a lip pursing
finger-lifting, tight-assed tea party. A real one.
The maddest of Mad-Hatter tea parties, and everyone's
invited. There's Curious George swinging
from the branches with Dumbo and Eeyore
and Horton, and little Cindy Lou Who cheering
them on. There's Homer Price and Tom Sawyer
and Christopher Robin making donuts like demons
and swapping tall tales with Sam I Am
and Miss Muffet and the Spider sitting down
beside each other and Snow White and Cinderella
and Sleeping Beauty comparing hair—and princes
and Tom and Jerry and Sylvester and Tweetie Bird
and even Wiley Coyote and the Road Runner laughing
so hard at their own cartoons that tears are coming
from their eyes and Hansel and Gretel and Dorothy
and the Scarecrow cheering for the death of wicked
witches and Roo and Kanga and Piglet shouting
hooray for the little engine that could

and Peter making Captain Hook walk the plank
while Tinker Bell shines from up on high and
all the fairy godmothers descend to give
their blessings at the end.

How does that sound? How does that compare with up?
So the next time someone yells at you, "Grow Up,"
just say—no thanks—I'm going for <u>down</u> or in
or back. Anything but up.

Time of Day

On the afternoon of Christmas day
the boy, triumphant, emerges like Mercury
from the RKO 86th St, corner of Lexington.
Filled with the gallantry of Gregory Peck,
he consults his new gold timepiece,
gift of the gods, wish fulfilled.

Twelve years old, he can sit without
his parents at the films. He knows the time
of day. Twenty after five. Dinner is at six.

"Excuse me, sir." A voice sounds at his back.
He turns and sees three boys, jacketed and scarved
against the cold, booted and bluejeaned,
smiling in the marquee's crystal light.

"Do you have the time?" the tall one asks,
The boy extends his wrist, enamored
of such a new and rich command.
"Beautiful watch," the second says.
"Can I see it?" asks the third.

The boy's nose smells skunk in the night
but arm extends despite itself. Hands
touch his wrist. "Wow," says the tall one
fixing his green eyes to the boy's blue.

Then they are gone, down 86th St. to Park,
boots scraping sparks on the cold cement.
The boy runs after them, club footed.

At six he sits at table, wrist bare,
head bowed. "Where is it, then?"
his mother asks. "What did you do?
Just take it off and hand it to them?"

IAN DONALD

Ian Donald is slight as a girl.
He wears round glasses with wire rims.
Ian Donald walks on his toes
and speaks without pronouncing
his r's. He makes English a's
broad as a hippo's belly.
"Pahk," he says, and "haht."

At recess we bump up against him.
We trip him and steal his shoe.
He cries, but we don't return it.
We throw it back and forth
over his head. We play football
with his shoe. We play baseball
and volleyball. Then we toss
the shoe in a mud puddle and walk
away. We don't look back.

After recess Ian Donald
shuffles into class with muddy knees
and snot running from his nose.
His eyes are red like pig's eyes.

Who did this? the teacher asks.
I want to speak but Terry
looks me into silence.

Someday I will speak out
and Terry will beat me up
behind the dumpster after school.
I will take the bright badge
of my bruised eye to Ian Donald
and then he will love me.

THE BOY, SEVENTEEN, VISITS HIS MOTHER IN THE HOSPITAL

His mother lies in the hospital bed
on Welfare Island. She lies in bloodstained
sheets in the hall because the rooms
are full. "Someone will die soon,"

she says. He sits, stiff and doomed
in the wooden chair beside her head.
He holds her cigarette while she puffs.
Between puffs she talks to him.

"They just took a look and sewed me up,"
she says. "I know it's cancer and they
couldn't do a thing. Don't tell your sister,
though. She isn't strong like you."

He feels a tightening of the throat,
a rising of the Nedick's hot dog
in his craw. He thinks of the evening
ahead and the monuments to Ruth

and Gehrig near the center-field wall.
If the ball rolls behind them, it's an
inside-the-park home run for sure.
"Don't let the bastards get you,"

she says. "They'll tell you things,
try to make you hate me. They'll say
I'm bad. Don't believe them, Toots."
"No, Mom," he says. "You're handsome,

Toots," she says, "and smart as hell,
but you could learn something about love."
She coughs and the grey pain takes her
under the eyes. "That was a bad one,"

she says, "kiss me, Toots, and go get
the nurse." Her smoke-edged fingers
touch his cheek, her dry lips brush
his own. He rises and walks down

the drab green hall to the narrow
nurse's window. No one there.
When he comes back his mother's eyes
are closed, and the long ash leans

dizzily on the ashtray's edge.
He smothers the remains on the sole
of his white-buck shoe. At the hall's
end the burning exit sign beckons.

Of Catchers
For Andy

in the rye and elsewhere I can only say
it is a matter of timing. These kids,
you know, running through the deep field,
not seeing the cliff and you there, noble you,
with your big hands grabbing one. Great.
But the next one tumbles screeching down below
into the whatever. The field is too damned
big, the kids are everywhere. You see?

Or the girl, the trapeze artist, swinging
her long legs out—once, twice, she flips
then grasping the rod behind her knees
back and forth, back and forth, she rocks
and launches out into the sweet nest
of your waiting hands.

                    But you, you're
swinging back, reaching now for air itself,
watching her fingers one last time stretching
for you as she falls.

                    Catching. It's bruised thumbs
and busted bones in every joint and a cold
smack in the soul every time you lose one.

So drop it, son, so to speak. Now.

Sandwiches

My dog eats only sandwiches.
I spread the Alpo like peanut butter
on the bread, plunk the pills
in the middle, then cut and feed.

He takes each bite with due
consideration, sweeping the dusty
floor with his tail. He chews
and swallows. I try to trick him.

I slip some Alpo on a plate
and hold it to his mouth. He sniffs
and turns away. For days now
he has held me in this grip.

Hot dogs, he had, then hamburgers,
chicken salad, but only with
the bread. What is it with bread?
Alpo is Alpo, with or without.

Myself I cannot fool.
Bread, I got plenty of. All kinds.
Pumpernickel, New York rye,
crackling Country Grain.

What's so great? There's no meat,
no stuff to go inside.
I know Alpo. I know air,
you can choke on only bread.

MY DOG, THE LOVER

seventy-five at least in human years
has fallen for a tawny, spaniel bitch
six houses down the street but uphill
all the way. He sits with other suitors

in the cool of her garage. He spurns
me as I drive by. I stop, clap my hands,
entreat him home with slurping sounds
of supper and hints of tummy rubs.

He stretches lazily, cocking an eye
at the black lab next to him as if to say
those humans are such bores. He rises,
lifts a leg to wet a dandelion, ambles

to the car and sits, head held high,
in the front passenger seat. At home
I let him out and turn my head to fetch
the groceries from the rear. Before I turn

again, he's gone, flashing up the hill,
this white haired Romeo on pads, tail out,
feathers fluffed. To hell with him, I say,
let him starve, let him feed on love.

Ten minutes pass. Thunder rumbles in the west.
I laugh and wait the count of ten. Sure enough,
like Mercury pursued by Mars, he races
to my side, Don Juan of dogdom, hiding his head
between my legs and trembling like a child.

WALKING THE DOG

The dog and I walk daily by the lidded
eyes of houses in our block, where spies

raise quietly the slats of old venetian
blinds to watch us limp in syncronicity

to the corner where he lifts his leg
in quiet ritual before we chance the gamut

of Main Street stores. I shop and he waits.
Sometimes when I come out, persons are fingering

his tags in disbelief that a such a scraggly
thing should be released for their inspection.

"Is this your dog?" they ask in tones
you'd save for perverts or ugly maiden aunts.

"Of course," I say, as we limp away
in harmony attained from years of calcifying

bones. "Is he sick?" the persons ask?
"No, only old," I answer, but I can tell

as I look back that they would have me up
for dog abuse if they could prove his strange

spasmodic gait was caused by masterly misuse.
"But he's so thin," they echo down the road

where we have stopped to greet some sweet
delicious smell. "Anorexic," I say gravely

then smile with special meaning. They cast
their eyes on high, appalled that men

with such neurotic traces should bring
their dogs to public places.

COLLEGE DAYS

It was the Harvard game, late October
leaves red and gold swirling on the ground.
Three stone stairways to Buzzy Krongard's
tower suite where black bartenders served
Ivy leaguers in tweed coats and ties.

Sharon James drank bourbon from four to six,
then disappeared on Buzzy's arm into
Scotty Larkin's bedroom. Her friend, Charlene,
who wasn't very cute, wondered where she'd
gone. We eased her fears with scotch

and lines from "The Waste Land." Later Buzzy
reappeared, his middle finger redolent
with musky woman smell. "She's ready,"
he said to several willing friends. I
excused myself and threw up in the hall.

That night when everyone had left
and she had walked with painful slowness
on her friend's arm into the growing
dark outside, I took them to the club
for supper as my guests, then sat with them

on the back porch under the green awning
watching the pattern of the falling rain
on the slowly turning trees. Sharon James
cried. Charlene patted her hand. For a long
time we drank coffee. No one spoke to us.

I see her still today, white thighs spread
among those sad discarded scarves on Scotty
Larkin's bed, I hear her lips say "no"
and I smell the finger of Buzzy Krongard
thrust under my nose.

SACRE COEUR: PARIS, CHRISTMAS EVE

1.

Eight young men, boys still in the brain,
full of blood longings, sperm longings,
ramble Paris streets in the December rain.

They are all virgins, first time away from home
fresh arrivals at St.-Lazare on the evening train.
Red-eyed from cheap white wine, thirsty for some

wild adventure of the night, they chug northward
speaking the names of places that they seek
in sacred whispers. "Pigalle," the leader says,

and from the others two by two the name "Pigalle"
erupts with gusty guffaws. "Moulin Rouge"
they say, "Berlioz" and "Boulevard Clichy."

Since thirteen they have dreamed these scenes—
bare-breasted women dancing behind gold fans,
black stockinged can-can girls from magazines

but most of all they look for prostitutes
with feathered hats and orange mini-skirts
for this is Paris and they are young

and tonight, by God, they will get laid.

2.

The one called James lingers in the rear,
a private prodded by his sergeant's stare.
"If it would only snow," he thinks in fear.

"If it would only snow and streetlights shine
and whores and pimps and racketeers come out
to play and celebrate the mystery of Christmas day

for it is dark and the rain drowns our souls
and Judas leers in alabaster robes
and God commands no voice." But he cannot

say no to their narrow need. Faster then
and faster the boys all speed. "Want ficky ficky,
boys?" the booted women plead. "Want ficky ficky,

nice little boys?" And now it seems to James
that they are rats shuffling on all fours,
sniffing and shoving their burning muzzles

against the bare legs in the hidden doors.
"There they are," the sergeant shouts, but James
is gone, running away toward the sacred heart

toward the beckoning white of the holy mount
past crimson wind-mill paddles, past penguins
in black coats who bleat "Come in, come in."

Up the thousand stairs his footsteps churn—
higher he climbs till flakes of falling snow
circle the dome and bless the streets below.

Lines Composed While Sitting in my Office, After Having Read Many Poems By My Fellow North Carolinians

They know the damp musk smell of earth in old
abandoned houses, the darkness of closed rooms,
flash of fish tail in frozen mountain streams,
lilt of blacktooth smiles in Appalachia.

They know the sudden lift of heron, crook-legged
before dusk and the way boys skip smooth stones
in still ponds. They know the lidless eyes
of snakes seen face to face across thin streams.

They know how dogs, tunneling for hermit crabs,
throw storms of sand into the startled air.
They know the skin of grandmothers, brittle,
like ancient maps hidden in attic trunks.

I know the faces of the young and the dark
stare in their lowered eyes when they have ceased
to hope. I remember how once in composition class
I sat easily on the desk, walking my words

like the afternoon dog, how suddenly the arms
and legs of a girl's voice tangled into the feet
of mine. Telling the garbled beads of her desperate
faith, she spoke to me in tongues. Glossolalia,

the word slipping from the lips like the sound
itself, her strangled cry for help from her unknown
God. Black girl, one of ten among four hundred,
tumbled into this spider world, begging for help,

Anthony S. Abbott

pressed into faith by a crippled man cruising
the freshman halls for converts, wrapping his web
round the pimpled and maimed, the different
and the ugly, promising eternal life in worlds

to come as recompense for scars in this one.
My class sits stunned and silent. The girl's
words slow. God, she says in English, has given
her permission to speak. "In all your classes?"

I ask. "No," she says, "just in this one."
I had heard of tongues only by the telling.
Now I am face to face. I dismiss the class,
walk her to her room and call the chaplain

who understands such things. She talks to me
of her faith with bits of tongue dispersed
between the lines. She will go home tomorrow
and we will never see her again.

THE DANCER SPEAKS TO HER EX-LOVER

Because I love to sing and dance
because my legs are long, my teeth are white
that does not mean my voyager soul
unfolds no sting, contains no bite.

Because I love to laugh and cry
because my hunter's eyes are bright
that does not mean I haven't breathed
the cat black terrors of the night

***

I am a miracle
every bone, every joint, every circled cell...
My fingers fold into fabulous conundrums
My brain makes pictures as bold and blue
as a thousand piece jig-saw puzzle
every part wondrously interlocked.

I am the tropical hibiscus
I bloom for a day then die
My color bursts on your eyes
like orange sunsets on distant skies
then fades into satin darkness.

So be it then. Let my day begin.
Let it be lived from the first breath of morning
to the last sigh of sleep. Let the tongue
taste the full five courses of the feast.

You, my would-be lover, offer me
the leavings of your modest plate.
You give me wilted greens
and warmed up chicken broth.
You send dried bread and water.

I am a miracle. My day is a feast.
I will drink the clear juice
of young coconuts. I will eat meats
with strange names. And I will have love.

Love so strong the tongue will taste
the soul of the beloved. My blood will course
with my lover's name. You offer me your
scraps.

I will have more. I will have life so rich
the very tips of my fingers will praise God.
I will live, my friend. So give me all
or go your own sad way. I am a miracle
and I will have it all.

NEWS STORY

A Clemson University student fell three stories to her death
Friday as she tried to inch her way along a narrow ledge
on the outside of a campus fraternity house, officials said.
Shannon Gill, 20, of Orlando, Fla., fell from the third floor
of the Alpha Tau Omega fraternity house at 1:10 a.m. as
she tried to climb along the 2-inch, rain-slick ledge, a univer-
sity spokeswoman said.

The Charlotte Observer, Dec. 9, 1989

A year now since Shannon Gill died
and still I mourn for her, still I think
of her each day as I pass the house
on my way to work. Sometimes I wake at night
and see the numbers on the clock framed
in the rain outside.
              I did not know her.
I did not even teach her. No excuse for tears
except the common one, and yet I cannot shake
her face, smiling, I believe, even at the end,
and the sorry unkempt look of the boy who still
today seems not to know what he has done.

They had been drinking, for a long time,
as the young do now, longer I think than we did,
less afraid to shake their bones in the Dean's eyes,
freer from whatever fear bound us to the side
of decency, brides to be who did not hide
what we sought, but bound our passion
in the twine of virginity's surprise.

They had been drinking, and hands on each other's
rears, they stumbled to the boy's third floor room,
hot for some release, and then the door locked,
key lost, the brother in the next room laughing.

Beowulf, Achilles those male paragons of boastful
virtue. Do it or you're not a man. Fine.
He'd done it before, walking the narrow
ledge from room to room to gain fame
if not access to a woman's arms.

Tonight the boy was scared. Drink
perhaps or the drops pounding on the freezing
ledge. But not Shannon. She was free, laughing,
one foot before the other, face flat against
the bricks, not a flinch, and the final look
a radiant smile before she goes like the last
of the diving birds flat out into the silent
night.

He never thought to hold her back. She was
a date maybe, someone fun for the night,
no pearl of great price.

Today I read the newspaper. Fourteen hundred
pilgrims have died, trampled, suffocated
in a tunnel to the holy city of Mecca. Bodies
piled upon bodies. King Fahd says the accident
was God's will. "If they had not died there,
they would have died elsewhere and at the same
predestined moment."

My stomach turns at his words. Such lies
to soothe the faithful. If them, why not
Shannon Gill? She might have been my daughter,
the boy my son. I reach out to hold you back,
Shannon,
but I catch only the withdrawing air.

FAR FROM HOME

Anthony S. Abbott

Far From Home

"Antonio, we're far from home, all of us are. Who's going to judge which of us has got the farthest way to go through all the shit and the dark?"
            —Leo Bebb in Frederick Buechner's <u>Love</u> <u>Feast</u>

But suppose you've <u>been</u> home and know
the very taste of home, not the bacon
frying taste, but soul taste, tongue
taste, and the touch, the very fingers
of home, the voice, cry in the heart,
clutch in the throat of home. Not
the pictures on the wall and mama's
apron strings, but the tooth smile
and the spirit swept into the last
row of peace and the head-shaking,
arm-swinging, foot-stomping, bone-rattling
shit-shaking taste of home.
                    I mean, suppose
you've known that, seen it, smelt it,
touched the very perfume of it, had it
in the billows of your gills, friend?

And then you got kicked out into the ice,
into the flat black frying pan of every day
and squatted in the grey brown grass
of what they call life and then some dude
who thought he knew something tried to save
you, tried to tell you what home was and how
to get there and you <u>knew</u> because you've
been, friend,— I mean, then, it gets tough
because what you had you remember like live
roses in winter, like fresh fish in an arctic
freeze. Like you know it, but you can't get
at it, and nobody cares because they don't
believe you know anything anyway.

Don't talk home to me,
friend. I've been there. And after that,
well after that, the world's just somewhere
to walk through. It looks pretty, it looks
like something— but under the red leaves
and the holly berries, you're still waiting
for home to come back and catch you in her
arms, as if she knew, as if she still cared.

Jesus Saves

1.

On the stall wall of the men's room
at Bojangles Restaurant some one has scratched,
"Fuck white men." Below it, another hand
has etched, "Fuck niggers." To the left,
in blue vertical letters a third has added,
JESUS SAVES. Three days to Christmas and my lips
burn with the taste of such exotic fare. "Good
for Jesus!" I yell to the wall. "Good for what?"
the sound bounces back, echoing, zigging
from ceiling to side, floor to dangling door.

I drive home. "Jesus saves," I announce
to the ribboned packages on the seat.
I hear the news. A motorist, drunk, at 3. a.m.
speeding the wrong way on the interstate
has crashed into a family driving south
killing all but a three year old boy.
"Jesus saves, Justin," I whisper to the radio.

But my heart is not in it. In Leninakan,
Armenia, children lie buried in their schools
and the sky over Lockerbie rains flaming
parts on lambs that sleep in thousand year
old barns. "Jesus saves," I shout to my
closed fist.

2.

Two days after Christmas and I dream.
I see a woman, a bride in high necked
dress, white with lace-work, pearls

everywhere. She stands before me, face
burned by some unknown fire, eyes buried
under layered sockets, holes only for ears.
Her hands are pig's feet, cloven. To Jesus
she is beautiful. I am supposed to kiss
her, but I am afraid. If I step too near
she will make me part of her forever.

3.

New Year's day and the incessant murmur
of football games, the tree unceremoniously
dragged through the back yard, silver icicles
trailing like reluctant strands of unruly hair.
Boxes packed and marked—angels, creche, Santa,
lights, ornaments—and once more the long walk
to the attic. "Jesus saves," I murmur as I close
the door.

4.

A week passes. Feast of the Epiphany. Paul
on the Damascus Road. I dream again. This time
a city, row houses, filthy across a street.
On my side a park. I sit in a car with no windows.
They come for me, men with dark skin, mustached,
hair greased down. Closer they come. They stop.
Look at me. The one in front spits, once, twice.

"I'm sorry," I say, wiping the spit from my face.
He laughs and his friends laugh. I fall crazily
from the car, twisting on the soft grass. I cry.
"I'm sorry," I sob. "I'm truly sorry." But he
only stands above and sneers. "Jesus Saves,"
he hisses, and I wake shaking in the silent dark.

Christmas Vespers

Grandfathers straining to hear, baby
sisters in starched petticoats, brothers
in unfamiliar ties, alien cars packed
along the leaf-strewn streets, they come
for the annual miracle as if the voices,
as if the bright-tongued girls and
ruby-throated boys could lift them,
touch them to eternity in this one
forgetting hour.

      No room in the inn,
I perch like a great horned owl
in the balcony below the organ loft,
hooting curses on all this holiness.
My gut aches tonight, and I cannot
listen for the pain.

      Once I too could make
tunes and see the smile of God in the
flickering candle's light. I too could
redraw time's face in the caverns
of my mind. I too could sing to asking
eyes of strangers and of friends.

Now, from my uneasy perch, I think
of shouting "Fire!" to watch them
tumble toward the doors in sudden fear.

Somewhere in the dark out there
the stable waits.

Longings

Once, years ago, I pricked my thumb
with a burnt pin and squeezed drops
of blood on a letter to my friend.

"Never do that again," she said,
and I didn't, but nights when earthsmells
thrust hard under the heart

I feel the urge to bleed once more,
to ride down the wrong side
of the road toward some rumbling truck

then pull up at the last and watch
the swerving driver's startled face
as I slide into the grass. It's dumb,

I know, but it beats moping. I like
to think of Henry the Eighth taking
off his shoes and walking barefoot

two miles and bloody to the shrine
of our Lady at Walsingham—to kneel
in the Virgin's house and beg a son.

And when she failed him he burned her
and tore her house to shards to fill
the empty places in his heart.

THE POET, THE LOVERS AND THE NUNS

I.

It is cool for June. The sky, shockingly blue,
aggravates the poet's dreams. He curses
the littered streets and the soft fingered
hustlers of the alleys. Shaking the rust
of solitude, he mounts the hill to the Cloisters.

The lovers are already there, twining their fingers
like the necks of swans on the gray stones of the parapets.
Their eyes shine with joy. The poet passes by.

Below, five sisters all in white emerge
from the Madison Avenue bus. In his mind's eye
the poet sees them, ducks in a row, their thin
black-stockinged ankles crossed in unison,
riding the tarred streets, mouths wide
at the blinding sights of the city's carnival.
Now they are safe, now they have come home.

II.

In Robert Campin's room the lovers laugh.
Their legs touch easily like old friends.
He whispers, she smiles and looks at Campin's
little man sliding on beams of light straight
toward the Virgin's ear. Out back, Joseph
makes mousetraps to catch the devil, while
the poet watches from the curving stairs.

III.

The sisters have found the room of the unicorn
tapestries. They are aroused. They chatter
gravely in muted whispers like children
after dark. The poet is angry. He cannot hear.

They are young. They carry their love for Christ
in the pockets of their hearts. They are white
with hope. Piece by piece they follow the hunt.
They taste the drool of hate in the hunters' mouths.
Bite and stab, bite and stab, bite and stab.
They cry silently within. It is their Lord,
their dearest God who bleeds for them.

All at once the smallest gives a startled
cry. She sees the flowered resurrection.
Her sisters gather near in watchful silence,
worshipping without words. The poet lurks
under the hunters watching.

IV.

The lovers have found "The Unicorn in Captivity."
They did not know that anything so beautiful
existed. Their hearts are the colors of flowers.
They see the face of God in each other's eyes.
Millefleurs say the French. A thousand flowers,
and somewhere there the lovers are lost. They are
past saving.

The poet thinks of politics. What use is art
if you're starving? After the revolution peasants
stormed the palaces and for fifty years the tapestries
warmed the tops of turnips and radishes,
beets and green beans. The poet likes the irony.

V.

The sisters are tired. They sit on the wooden bench
facing the fragrant garden. They breathe the scent
of summer herbs. All in white, they watch the sky.

The lovers rest opposite them against the stone.
He cradles her in his arms, covers her eyes. They are
suspended in the slant whispers of nodding leaves.

The poet is sick. He has seen too much.
He misses the sound of horns in the checkered
streets. He boards the A train, downtown side,
Graffitied posters are manna to his eyes.

Anthony S. Abbott

LE MONT ST. MICHEL

Only a saint could live here. Even in May
wind from the sea ices the blood. I stand
in the Marvel trying to warm my hands

and I think of the monks who copied
in this room with fire to thaw the ink
and their freezing fingers. I wonder

what faith drove them across the sand
dragging leaden caskets for penance?
What faith hauled the slow stones up

the reluctant hill to the holy place?
Today the fast cars line the dry causeway.
The waters of the Red Sea vanish into time.

The tourists stand in line for Ma Poulard's
famous stew. They lick strawberry tarts
from their lips. Yet still the place is holy

and still we struggle up the steps. My sister
gasps for air and old ladies in print dresses
sit on the stones too stubborn to go down.

Yet still we come for signs, looking alone
from stone benches, searching the sea where
soldiers passed thirty years ago to make

white crosses on the beach called Omaha.
Michael, warrior saint, watched them
from his spire. And I, in the Marvel, watch

the wind rattle the glass. I wonder what
the old monks wore under the brown-grey gowns.
I wonder why they came, who watched, or watches still.

VEZELAY

*In 1569 the church was sacked by the Huguenots during the
religious wars of the Reformation.... Here the Huguenots amused
themselves by playing a macabre kind of lawn bowls with the
severed heads of monks against the faces of still living monks
buried to their necks as markers.*
Melvin Hall, <u>Bird</u> <u>of</u> <u>Time</u>

So says my cousin Melvin, who lived on the hillside
below the church for many years, and I believe him, religious
manners being what they are. We are no

better nor no worse. Wouldn't God Bless 'em our
red blooded blue jeaned tractor capped Jesus loving born in the
USA Americans do the same to Ayatollah

and his friends, if they could? Maybe God left something out
when he made us. Where did this religious one upmanship
come from?

The Church of the Madeleine at Vezelay was big
time for a while. Bernard of Clairvaux and Richard
the Lion Heart preached here. In the twelfth century

the little town on the hillside numbered twelve
thousand souls. Why? Because some enterprising monk stole
the bones of Mary Magdalene from an Abbey

down the road. We're number one, say the monks
at Vezelay, until later on the monks in Aix
find better bones. Vezelay stands disgraced.

Their bones are fake. Surely it's a joke. No,
The people don't think so. During the Revolution
all over France they lop the tops from statues.

Headless saints multiply like Saint-Denis, who
carried his decapitated face from the Mount of Martyrs
for many miles, so they say.

CHARTRES REVISITED: TO A CRITIC

No-I hate "France-poems." Besides, it's sentimental
and depends on a lot of easy adjectives.
     — Anonymous critic of a poem about Chartres

I picture you, crouched in a student union
upstairs, poems scrunched up before you
by hundreds, like shells of onion skins.

Your pen scratches with rage. "No—unmoving,"
you write with clear exacerbation. "No—
lacks the emotion it needs." Oh God

you shape the words with such deceptive ease.
Chartres, Vezelay, Mont St. Michel dismissed
like cattle branded in a gate. Next please.

I had wanted only to tease you into seeing
. the glory of the South Rose Window on Easter
eve, lights off, candles snuffed, nothing

but the shift of sun in April staring behind
and the walls so black they seem the boundaries
of hell itself— and in the midst color and glass

floating blue and white in the circled light,
the silence deep as love, the German guide gone
to buy beer in the local pub, the travelers

shifting in crowded seats on the Paris train.
Outside, in the darkening west the gallery
of kings grey with the day's age, my host and me

nearly alone on this deserted stage, old man
paralyzed in leg and arm, staring with his one
good eye at the center of the Rose—Christ eternal,

angels, elders, beasts chanting songs of praise.
My host dreams of latter days when limbs will be
made whole, when souls and bodies mix in perfect

harmony and peace. Then suddenly the sun gives way
and the dark slides through the colored glass
like life expiring. Unexpected tears take the old man.

I rise and wheel him westward under the shape
of Jesse's rising stem, westward past Christ
enthroned in stone, out into the cobblestone street.

"Tres belle," I murmur to the old man's ear,
the only French I have. He gurgles some strange
laughter. "Oui," he says, "Ah, oui, tres belle."

Sancta Camisia

In the year of Our Lord 876 Charles the Bald—
grandson of Charlemagne—celebrated his return
from Jerusalem by presenting to the Cathedral

at Chartres a piece of cloth supposed to have
been worn by the Virgin Mary at the birth
of Jesus. Perhaps he was taken in by Arab traders

who after all have supplied susceptible Christians
for centuries with crosses, thorns, and loincloths
enough to perform the crucifixion hundreds of times.

Still, Sancta Camisia, as it is called, has been
certified by scientists as first century, and even
today, despite the Reformation and the noble efforts

of the French Revolution, pilgrims flock to kiss
the glass of the holy cloth, and on feast days
the lame are carried in leather litters to light

their candles before it. Senseless, say the scoffers,
but not I. I say it's a damn clever way of making
money. The Bishop of Chartres, who dragged it

from the fire in 1194 used it to pry from pious
people a whole new church. Sancta Simplicita.

Anthony S. Abbott

Ely Cathedral: Toward Evensong

Not dusk but its semblance, rain making
the stones cold, March damp, gray sky
blanketing both towers, only the greenness
of grass hinting at July. We shuffle through
western doors, umbrellas dripping. Another
day, another page in the Baedeker.
My wife drifts to the tearoom to warm
her hands. She will read her romance.

I walk down the painted nave expecting little.
Too many days, too many aisles, too many Norman
arches. I remember the words of my professors.
Clerestory, I murmur, and triforium. My head
knows the beauty of these forms, but heart
has flown to landscapes of home. I kneel
in a front pew and close my eyes. I speak
the names of absent friends. I call up faces.

From somewhere music. Beyond me, in the choir,
boys rehearse for evensong. "Kyrie," they sing,
"Kyrie eleison." "Christ have mercy," I echo,
"have mercy," and all at once I see—not boys—
but wheelchairs circling the altar before me,
wheelchairs with children of all ages, who cannot
speak or move their limbs. Muscleless, they sprawl,
heads propped by braces, eyes crossed absently.

I am frightened. My heart beats wildly. In the
choir the boys sing again, their voices pure
as night before first light, while one by one
attendant women turn the children's heads upward.
They point to the light above and all at once
mind and eyes remember the octagon of Ely
and those giant beams of oak hoisted to hold
the glass of the lantern and the eight-pointed

of the Carousel

d, mother. Do you remember
ode the winged horse?
w we rode through the night
e cries into the dark,
ur arm around my knees, one
other reaching, reaching
horse, Pegasus, you said,
y, and you laughed, mother,
ll of my back, and said,
will grow," and I did,
grew. Now my breasts push
my thighs squeeze the wooden
p and down, up and down,
, and I reach, mother,
nly your sad laughter
hat push for life
of the rotted park.

golden star which binds the dome. The children
hear the music, see the cunning of the craft,
the many fingered dome, they sense as I cannot,
the painted hand of God. My eyes swim, knees
ache from the dense wood. I look again into
the lantern's light and down into the children's
eyes. What do they think? Do they ask why God
creates such wondrous sights and helps them

not at all? Do they scream within? I butt
my head against the kneeling rail and watch
their eyes again and the soft hands of the nurses.
Ask them, says my better self, but my lips
spell only silence, legs stalk awkwardly away.
In the bookstore I will read of Etheldraeda,
saint of Ely isle, who married twice
and still remained intact. That will be good.

ON SEEING SAINT JOAN ONCE AGAIN

For Lindy Wood

"O God that madest this beautiful earth, when will it be
ready to receive Thy saints? How long, O Lord, how long?"
Epilogue to Saint Joan

The maid flashes fire. Her eyes burn with soul.
The vein in her neck throbs with God's sweet
dream, and her lips make words that heaven
has taught her. Only her body is here, and even
that lunges toward paradise. The others bumble
after truth, like ants on an afternoon picnic.
They know nothing. At the end she stands alone
whispering to her God in somber muted silence.

The audience files out. A man in blue, bloated
like logs long in water, passes me. "Boring,"
he says to his companion. "Asshole," I answer.
The word is out before the man has passed.
"It's you who are boring, you cretin!" I cry.
"Fool! bug-eyed, blasted, stupid fool!" I shout.
I crush my program, throw it in his face
and dash for the door. Outside in the alley
My eyes flash fire. I scrape my fingers
on the theater wall till blood runs. I ask
forgiveness for myself and take the grey pain
for penance.

The Girl Spea

Bellerephon, you
that? The hero wh
Do you remember
air, lights leaping
you standing with
hand on the pole,
for the ring, and t
winging out and a
your smile in the s
"Wait, little one, y
mother. I grew an
against the pole ar
sides, as we bump
into the plotted da
but there is no ring
mocking the leaves
against the dry du

with wine, bridges over the Seine, whispers
at night as the train winds whitely into Swiss
hills. She feeds you from her mouth, sings
into your soul. Your heart warms darkly to her song.

3.

I wait, like an old bear after winter sleep.
I prowl the halls, scratching my back on the closed
doors. Inside, voices drone like my grandfather's
Evinrude. Students drool on their notes, pencils

clatter to the floor, elbows slipping sidewise
heads bouncing off the rude desks. You laugh. Good.
I move from room to room. Invisible, I peek.
Nothing here but shoes and the shapes of old notes.

Nothing here but sad backward moments
of texts untaught. You know. Good. Mark it with blood.
You'll make a teacher. She'll have you all right.
She loves the daring, the hungry, and the young,

askers of hard questions, senders of messages
in bottles, sleepers under the open air. And me?
I still scratch and growl under the leaves,
searching for that further spring.

Anthony S. Abbott

THE MUSE IS ANGRY

The muse is angry. She turns her back. She stands
hands on hips, her face a picture of disgust.
I am mute. My mouth makes soundless shapes,
My tongue thickens. I mumble cliches through
swollen gums. She laughs and mounts her horse,
riding toward the hills with the skill of centuries.

I grope for my horse. He is fat with yellow teeth
and soured smile from years of toting dudes.
He bites my toe as I mount, thrusting my groin
awkwardly against the horn. We jerk forward like old
films staggering through ill set sprockets.

The insides of my calves burn. My backbone
shudders from the rattle of his ill timed canter.
And I remember how I could ride once—bareback,
gripping the reins and mane as one, lying almost
on the horse's neck, catching his rhythm in my knees.

The muse laughs at me like Hawthorne's Pearl,
"Thou wast not bold! Thou wast not true!"
And I am Arthur Dimmesdale hand on heart
limping through the darkening streets of Salem.
"Begin again," she says, and I write, "The muse
is angry..."

THE MUSE IS SULLEN

The muse is sullen. She turns from me, tucking
her legs tight to her chin. She leaves me
to stare at the brown moles high on her back.
I swear revenge in crimson fury. I will write

no more. I will find another. I will do damage
to myself, I plead to her shoulders. I run
into the dark street, hoping she will follow.
I stumble over the lids of empty garbage cans

scraping my knees on the grid of old cement.
I run to her door, crying for her to kiss
the hurt and make it well. Inside all is strange.
"Sit down," she says like the green sea at evening.

And I sit and listen to her tales of life under
the waves. I forget my hurt and the sound of her
old voice, distant and thin like old men's hair.
For the new is rich like the folds of bird's wings.

I see for the first time the color of her gown
and the small inscriptions on her bracelet. Fine
lines crow from the corners of her eyes. And her
fingers move like music to the rhythm of her words.

THE MUSE IS SILENT

The muse is silent.
    Her dark hair twisted,
        she stands in the corner

of my room, looking past the treetops
    to the moon. I frame
        her face with the shelved books

and the treetops to make
    an image. It is easy,
        I think, to write thus.

I lick the end of my pen.
    "It is dark," I begin,
        "and the slick branches

Of the slighted trees
    dance crazily in the winter wind.
        The moon is ice.

She freezes my veins in slow
    gray strokes. One brown
        leaf flutters earthward."

I pause and read my words.
    The muse is silent.
        Her dark hair twisted,

She stands in the corner of my room,
    smiling. It is easy,
        I think, to write thus.

THE MUSE HAS GONE

The muse has gone, departed for regions westward.
I flush through drawers for old poems. I seek
solace from French postcards. I read letters
from discarded lovers and place their words,
slightly altered, in obscure forms on the page.

I play Larry Bird with the local wastebasket,
lofting paper hookshots from right and left,
popping three pointers from the far corner
where Milton rests with Donne, Herbert and Traherne.
Exhausted, I sit. From my neighbor's room

The sound of voices. I picture him. Tall, easy,
pipe in mouth, blue oxford, button down. He speaks
with the voice of God mellowed by Old Forester.
Easy, sure as Shakespeare on a spring night
in Stratford. He talks. His student listens.

This is good, he says, that is not. Do this,
he says, and all will be well. Read this,
not that. The student questions. He answers.
Terror lurks in my throat. He knows. Blessed
God, he knows. Do this, he says, and all will

be well. In alarm I close the door, but still
I hear the sounds, calm, full of smoke and patched
elbows and the smell of wine and old leather.
My room swirls, a thousand books unhinged. And I
look westward. The muse has gone. The muse has...

Anthony S. Abbott

Silence

Early evening. A thousand starlings darken
the sky. They fly, shrieking, to the tops
of my pines. In her kitchen, my shrill-voiced
neighbor hears them, tumbles, frying pan
in hand to the deck's edge, hurling curses,
pounding pan with wooden spoon, frightening the birds
from their new perches to farther trees
across the bay. But speech is endless. The starlings
squall long into the night like strangers in airplanes,
like children on schoolbuses in a new snow,
like college boys in bars after football games.
They all speak at once, holding drinks in their
thin black wings. They wink like gulls on fences
and go on shrieking. No one listens. Words tumble
terribly in the narrow dark out over the grey bay.
I think that each word spoken is a poem lost.

WORDS

multiply like sociologists
    like white rats manufactured
        in Durham, North Carolina
            for professional use only

stream from smiling mouths of coiffured
    television commentators asking so easily
        "how do you feel about the burning
            of your business, Mr. Nicely?"

Old men with large bellies stand on sidewalks
    poking their fingers at one another's chests
        speaking of God with the ease of friends
            speaking of hell with clear familiarity

speaking of the volts on Florida's electric chair
    and the latest rape headlined in the Daily News.
        I am frightened of these words. They are like frogs
            slipping from lips of creatures on late, late shows.

From the doors of boardrooms, from the Pentagon's hull,
    from the crenelated towers of the Kremlin
        to the wounded streets of Manila and San Salvador
            men shout, "I am good and my enemy is evil!"

Why are they all so sure, so cock green certain?
    What do they know that I do not? What do they see?
        I see white ice on winter ponds and green fields
            of corn where frightened children hide.

My mouth opens, but I speak only silence, I speak
    the imagined notes of violins and cellos.
        Is it not better? I do not know, but I think
            yes.

STONE SOUP

The cauldron beckons stones,
the soldier says, laughing.
Tooth mother knows the game.

Stones plop solidly down,
then carrots, beans, beef,
red, bleeding from the sides

of slick brown cows. Corn,
say the boys, and golden
ears press down with sprouts

and slotted heads of cabbages,
yams and squash and bristly
 hair of broccoli. The mother

stirs and smiles and blesses
with her shifting eyes
such rich forgotten stew.

The boys eat and swell.
They grow like Polyphemus
all in grit and muscle.

The artist alone eats stone
And spits the sand of his craft
into the eyes
of the astonished world.

ANOTHER KIND OF SECRET

The shape of a poem
   is the face behind
      the space which hides the eyes.

There are words unspoken
   or spoken slantwise
      by the sly mouth.

If I write, "The thin stalks
   quiver in the field
      above the fish pond"

or "roses are cold hope
   for stones"
      or yet again

"On the night she died
   her skin shone gold"
      you must not stop with sound.

You must trace the poem's face
   with the tips of your fingers
      and flush truth's white dove

from her sweet hiding place.
   For only when she flies
      will you see her wings.

WORDS ARE THE ONLY FINGERS
OF THE SOUL

1.

I wake at five in the morning
        full moon shining on the lake
                and think of you swimming

In your own thick waters
        buoyed up by that absurd faith
                I have never had that whatever

lurked, slippery, in the green deep
        wished you no harm.
                This has always been your hour,

too bright for night, too still for dawn
        when nothing is either right or wrong
                but simply, beautifully, *is*.

I try to place you. I grope
        through the atlas, state by state,
                searching the name of your town

the numbers of highways
        as if names and numbers like talismans
                could roll the rock from your door.

Words are the only fingers of the soul
        words spoken and heard
                written and received

like hands thrust deep into bowls
        of ripe cherries, then pulled,
                burgundy stained, into the air.

2.

I see you now as a child of nine
         riding the thin mountain road
                 in your father's Ford,

hill steep, tight with laurel on one side,
         the other a bank falling down, down
                 and suddenly three wild ponies

bolt before your eyes—roan, dapple, black—
         I don't know, I must invent,
                 and the father, angry, pushing

obscenely down on the reluctant pedal,
         ponies, eyes in panic rolling
                 like your own, and your words

"Please, Daddy, please," the car closing
         the manes waving, sweat on their haunches
                 small feet kicking dust

and the ponies sliding, tumbling over the side
         in your mind's eye
                 or smashing blood-full

into the Ford's grill, the father laughing,
         maybe, as you scream
                 and cover your eyes

fingernails cutting the skin
         above your blond brows
                 drawing blood.

Then, an opening, unforeseen,
         the ponies veer, vanish
                 into the thick dark green

and the father unrelenting still
        points the snarling car
                downward to hellmouth.

        3.

We thirst for news
        we die for want of story.
                Tell me more, the heart cries.

I know now when you make the horse noise
        in the throat you are one
                with your wild sisters

open mouthed in their flawless pain.
        We are one with the animals, you say.
                I know, I understand. I see

you dancing, breasts free, feet bare
        skirts swirling, hair fresh
                washed from the summer lake

in that wilder wood of your imagining
        neighing under the maddening moon
                while my fingers write these words.

THE MOLE FLOWER

THE MOLE FLOWER

*To the memory of Jeanne Sarver,
Joey Tesh, and Leslie Walker*

1.

Rain again today, unseasonably cold
for the end of May, mist rising off the lake,
headlights snaking down the Interstate,
the only sign of bright in these unending

shades of grey and grey. I stay in the slow
lane, tacking northward to see my son
away at school, flinching as tractor trailers
spread waves of spray across my fragile bow.

I stop to breathe and watch the green leaves
shake against the wind. It is too soon
to drive, too soon since Friday afternoon
the heavy yellow bus crawling on legs

too slow across the busy road, struck
broadside by the rushing truck—hurled,
curled around the throat of a hundred
year old willow oak, three children

dead— two girls, thirteen, yearning to wear
their mothers' clothes for the first time,
a boy confirmed in church five days before—
quiet ones from the middle of the bus.

2.

Their cries hurl stones in God's face,
but from the sky only silence looms, quiet
as winter ice. Once we all asked why,
thrust our burning tongues into the open

mouth of space, demanding to know truth.
We are wiser now, carriers of flowers not
of bricks. Roses ring the oak tree's base,
roses and yellow gladiolas. A foil balloon

strains on its string in the twisting rain.
I bring the mole flower, child of my own
imagining, with center warm and brown
pulsing of earth and the wet tips of noses

under the furrowing ground. I bring the mole
flower, with petals purple and white, flower
of the three day sleep and the rolled stone.
I place it gravely on the tree's scarred side

and grieve in the winnowing wind.

3.

My car still sprays through the grumbling storm.
I squint at the road through the slicing blades.
In the churches mourners gather to pay tribute
to the dead. They speak their names in hesitance

and pain. Jeanne, they say, and Leslie and Joey.
They remember certain street corners and sounds
from outside on autumn mornings. Then suddenly
they see the fire of the new ascended saints

rising, rising into the darkening skies.
Inside my car, the mole flower glows. Rain
is everywhere, but I splash on through the puddled
streets. We have been saved for something.

The Beginning

"It isn't the end that's important," said Mary. "It's the beginning."
                    Romulus Linney, <u>Jesus</u> <u>Tales</u>

You see, I have forgotten everything
except the loving. I do not know
about the kissing, the placement
of the hands or the lips or whether
the tongue goes this way or that.

I do not know any more about the touching
or the movement of limbs
or the freedom of the eyes to watch
or whether anything is wanted
or how one knows desire. I remember

only that on certain nights
when the full moon hung low on the horizon
there was the beginning
of something more than you and me
something more than self

and if I lost that forever
it would be losing God
or whatever God is. To save that
I would perform a a hundred tasks
pluck a thousand blossoms,

do penance under some saint's rock
if only it would lead
to a blue door in the green wood.
I would unlive it all
so we could again begin.

ON THE SECOND DAY

Today the bride wears her wedding dress
to the picnic on the rocks by the stream
which flows south from the Roman church
where she spoke her vows the day before.

She hitches her train with one hand, shows
a bare leg to the admiring groomsmen
then wades ankle deep in the clear mountain
water. The father, who had wept walking

the girl down the pocked stone aisle,
trembles to see the sun shine on her fine
black hair, and a boy in shorts wades to her
with champagne, bowing profusely in the little

rapids. She turns with a radiant smile and toasts
us all. She would like to be a bride forever.

DUST BENEATH MY SHOE

Her marker rests beyond the centerfield fence
under a mulberry tree. The boys once, chasing
a long home run, found the ball nestled near
her name. I had not told them where she was,
for they had come later and we had shrouded
the sad past, buried her beyond the lawns
of their green memories. They knew of her,
of course, and stared with inward eyes, tracing
the shapes of the letters with their fingers.

The dirt of place marks the patterns of our lives.
"Where you from?" the natives ask with the slow
drawl and easy sense of ownership only time
in Southern towns can bring. "From here," I say.
They smile, knowing the accent is foreign,
and ask again, slyly, "Where'd you <u>come</u> from?"

"New York," I say, when my daughter rests blessedly
only a boy's throw past the centerfield fence,
and thirty miles down the old highway to Charlotte
in the city cemetery, mother and grandmother lie
in unmarked graves. New York is good enough, where
mother, lonely for grandmother's ghost, died in '51
and shuttled down the narrow hall of memory into—
for all I knew and cared— nothingness, until one day,
like the boys, quite by accident, I found her name
in the register—Frances Hayden Covington— Faith,
Hope and Charity, she used to say— of the old public
cemetery down the road.

"Where you from?" they ask again, knowing no Charleston
cousins or Spartanburg aunts, knowing the car stays
in the gravelled drive on holidays. "From here," I say
to the dust beneath my shoe. And still they ask,
"But where'd you <u>come</u> from?"

Anthony S. Abbott

REMEMBRANCE

"Nothing hurts as bad as they say it does...and clear, pure memory doesn't hurt at all. What hurts is forgetting.... Remember everything."

Josephine Humphreys, <u>Rich</u> <u>in</u> <u>Love</u>

The spring rises from the earth, root to stem
blossom to leaf. Each day catches the breath
like a song remembered, forgotten then found
again. In a night the Bradford pears turn
white to green and tulips splash in haunting
reds by my neighbor's door.

You rise like the season. Your face shines
in the pools along the road as I walk
to the grave yard. I pass the old house.
You glide down the stairs and take my hand.
We share the season. Is it hyacinth or lilac
I smell? I lie in the grass beside your stone.
I watch the bees work in the crossed branches
of the blooming apple tree. The sky shines beyond.

I bring you my anger and my pain. I hand
them to you like bread. I speak the loaves
of my sorrow, the broken pieces of my rage.
I have beaten the trees in my back yard wood
till my hands turned blue from gripping
the pounding stick. I have known knuckle
blood and screams in the soundless throat.

Now I hug the earth, pressing my chest to the growing
grass, spreading my arms outward. I close my eyes
and wait. The anger drains like water after rain.

You smile at my smallness, you kiss my folly
with your parted lips. "Sit," you say,
and I squat with you cross-legged like some
novice guru. "Kneel," you say, and the stone
cuts the letters of your name into the memory
of my knees. "Eat," you say, and my mouth opens
like the yawning bird's. "Taste," you say,
and your sugared love charms the buds of my tongue.

I rise like one groggy after dreaming. I stagger
homeward on the cracked sidewalk into the back yard
of the old house. Everywhere, in the knee-high grass
spring flowers bloom madly.

Apple Blossoms

All day I have thought about apple blossoms
how there are no apple blossoms here
yet even so I am standing in an orchard
my hands reaching toward them
and they are not apple blossoms at all
but dogwood, white dogwood,
and I feel in my hands the imprint
of the nails and the shape of the cross.
It is spring, and everywhere there are blossoms,
dogwood, flowering cherry and azaleas close
to the ground. I pluck flower after flower
my arms groaning with the wet blossoms
and you are not there.

The others are so young when I give them
branches. They look at me with such gratitude.
I kiss them lightly on the lips
I hold them and feel their hearts
beating. But they are not you
and at night they carry their blossoms
to young men.

NIGHT CRAZIES

"What man among you if your son asked
for bread would give him a stone."
Matthew 7:9

If I placed a stone in your hand and said
"This is my body," would you believe me?
And would the stone, indeed, be my body
because I spoke it and you believed it so?

At night I ask myself such questions
while my husband sleeps, in the next bed, the TV on,
mouth open, yellow pencil in hand,
the Times crossword on lap
bifocals over nose
head tilted toward water glass
on bedside table. Sometimes, before he dozes,
he asks for down and across, but I know nothing
of use to him. Instead, I think. . .

If gave you bread and said, "This is my body,"
would it indeed be. . . ?

I remove his glasses
I watch the nose hairs quiver slightly as he breathes,
then walk barefoot to the porch.

I look for owls in the back yard oak. I think of God.
Fire and tongues. Tongues of fire. Disciples burning
at Pentecost. My English teacher says that loving God
is like coming.

My husband says bullshit. My husband says that English
teachers only want to seduce you. I read Proust
in the mornings at the public library. "Elle glissait
dans ma bouche sa langue." She slid into my mouth
her tongue. How wonderful of that the sound.

I have forgotten how to kiss, where the nose goes,
the feel of tongues on the inside of the lip.

My English teacher says I should write poems.
He likes the rhythm of my words. My husband wants me
to work. We could retire in ten years and live
off our joint income.

They are starving in El Salvador
but we only send them guns. The Russians and the Cubans
send them guns.
I would give them our joint income for food.
My husband says I have no will. He does.
The aorta is damaged. He takes it out

and replaces it with nylon. Can you repair genius?
They rebuild the arms of baseball players
and the new arms are better than the old.

Can you rebuild souls?

My husband says only faggots and horny, middle-aged
ladies write poems. "Pomes," he calls them.
I've got a great body, he says. I should model.
"Give up this poetry shit," he says, putting his hand
between my legs. I turn away.

My English teacher's right. Loving God _is_ like coming.
Without passion neither one is any good.
My soul's a stone. Can Jesus make bread from stones?

When I was sick, when they had me in their white bed
the nuns circling round smiling
and Jesus over me staring down from the wall
I couldn't watch his eyes. I took kleenex
from my bag and covered him.
The nuns took it off. I covered him again.

Take me hard or take me not at all. That's the point.
I can't make him take me. I can't make the stone bread,
I can't. . .

I see the bike leaning against the oak.
Do it, my heart says. I see myself, robe
over my head like some celestial creature's cape,
gown hiked above the thighs, wheels spinning
through the rat black dark, windows lidded
this crazy lady flying down the streets
at three a.m.

I laugh out loud and walk to the door
feet cold in the damp night grass. Nice, nice
I like it, but my knees buckle.
I slump beside the bike against the tree
feeling the rough lined bark against my back.

I scrape my skin against the grain
up and down then up again
when you make your own pain, it's different.

When the tears come, you choose them,
you choose them, but not yet. I hold them back, feeling
for the blood on my back, smelling the tips
of my fingers, clearing my brain.

Anthony S. Abbott

Jesus says he came to save us, but only if we lose
ourselves for him. We hedge our bets with beds
and boats and locks. Is it bread or a stone?
Is it his body or not? Who dies for stones?

Maybe death's the way. Tomorrow, at noon perhaps,
on the main street, a child, toddler, bolts
from its mother's grasp, chasing a dog,
yes, good, chasing a dog into the path. . .
yes, and I dive headlong, cradling the child
against my womb.

But could I, or would I stand and stare?
It is, you will admit, an answer, an act
of passionate definition, you might say.

I laugh, come back to myself under the oak,
my fingers barked and bloody. In the morning
my husband will ask where the blood came from
and I will say that I don't know.

POEM FOR ANNE

Catholic boys in Belfast
are taught by ten to make
grenades and throw them
at passing British soldiers.

Girl children learn the arts
of destruction more reluctantly
preferring at times even play
with Protestant acquaintances.

I am so sick these days
of the barbarities of men,
belly laugh in the pub slyly
covering the spit and snarl

bearcuff network of good
old boys, slam of brakes
and the muffled cries of battered
women in the dark. Then I think

of you weeping for Willy Loman,
pounding your fists bloody
on the classroom wall for those
who died at Auschwitz, and I wonder

if women, freed from the stain
of their black bonds, may catch
us too in their fierce fires.
We are only what we learn.

TURTLE

1.

Is a turtle without its shell
only a very thin man walking down Broadway
in the middle of winter with no clothes on?

Or is shell itself so much the essence
of turtleness that even the idea of without
is absurd— like clicking sticks silently?

Or is the mind too small
trapped in its own perceptions
caught in the narrow gauge

of muscle and vein and blood
unable to conceive the mystery
of you and me?

2.

It begins with me pushing
flesh riven from flesh
head up, neck stretching

You calling, "Carpe Diem" or some such nonsense
me scared shitless
hiding in the honey pot of shell

but pushing, still pushing upward
till the eyes see over the hump
a world not bound, not fixed

by the limits of brown bone.
    Ah, the shoulders, the shoulders
        and the arms raised high

like some grizzled, ancient cheerleader
    before the walls of Troy
        watching the heels of Hector in the dust.

Now the hard part, the waist
    and those unmentionable privates
        and you smiling somewhere I cannot see

watching me, half crawling, half walking
    on my blistered hands, feet and knees
        still inside, some monstrous mix

of man and beast until I flip and fall
    scraping my newly minted back
        on the pebbled road, feeling the goad

of my own blood for the first time
    and reaching, God, reaching, touching
        myself with my own fingers

and the eyes alive to color and shape
    the feet feeling earth, knobby
        old knees trying to lock, trying

to hook the body up, but the whirl
    beginning, dizzying purples
        and reds swirl round and round.

3.

It is not, of course, a dream
　　and later I see your shell
　　　　a quarter-mile beyond.

It takes a while, putting one foot
　　in front of the other
　　　　learning how the toes work.

I get there by singing
　　some song you taught me
　　　　in the cradle of the other life.

I tap on the front door— nobody home
　　and from the next hill I hear
　　　　the silver of your laughter.

CARROT COLORED WORDS
For Kappa and Jay

The dialogue goes something like this:
"I love you," I say, it being the end
of our conversation. "I love you,"
you sigh weakly after long silence.

I challenge your desultory reply.
"It's the word," you say. "It's been
overused. We need to find a better."
I accept the task. For nights I search

for carrot colored words, for words
with tails and purple horns and long
red sashes round their middles. I scream
for green words with yellow spotted stomachs.

My doctor friend tells me how patients
miss medical terms. A woman in Georgia
spoke of suffering from "Smiling Mighty
Jesus," meaning spinal meningitis.

Another had "Fireballs of the Eucharist,"
in reality fibroids of the uterus. If I
could choose, I'd take Jesus too. And those
fireballs beat fibroids all to hell.

That's the kind of word I want. I fireball
you. I smiling mighty Jesus you. It's cute
and satisfies your need for something new
but it's not exactly what I mean to say.

Anthony S. Abbott

What I mean to say is—if I was dying
and I could choose one person in the world
to sit and hold my hand and hear whatever
words I had to say—it would be you

and I know no better term for that
than love. If I find one, I'll let you know.

THE LEGENDARY STILLNESS OF HERONS
for Emily Abbott Nordfeldt (1900-1989)

I.

You hover in blue over the places of our souls
like some household saint, covering our daily
tasks with your wise laughter. "Pooh," you say
to the sugared mush of our sentimental talk.

"I love you, Emily," we write in our letters.
"I love you, Emily," we tongue to the open
mouths of our telephones, but you know
the hard edge of love and the horn of giving.

You wait like snow in spring in the high
mountains for the blossom of our steps
for the early greening of our voices.
We sleep in the valley of our forgetfulness.

At the end you know. You gather the cloak
of your going. Your friends wait. Your favorite
dog sleeps on the bed beside you. The pictures
of your parents beckon you to come. Your eyes

close. The long pain of crippled knees
and the brown indignities of age vanish
in the gratitude of death. Three days
later out of time your Easter lily blooms.

II.

Finally we come, like street urchins
kicking our guilt before us into the empty
rooms. We walk blind, fingers for eyes,
and touch the remembrances of our hearts.

Objects resonate with life. White china birds,
a gray stone horse, paintings of afghans,
possums, porcupines and ponies, a silver headed
cane, a book which bears the giver's name

inscribed to you at Christmas thirty years before,
photos of our chidren curled and bent
tucked in drawers or propped on porcelain lamps.
My oldest sister stands before the garden door

eyes bright in the miracle of memory.
I reach to touch her hand then stop, myself
transformed by her voyaging mind. I see us
hauling a hand-hewed tree from the far field

the Christmas of my fourteenth year. You smile
at my silly questions. We don't BUY decorations,
we are artists. We make our own with paper
and glue and tufted cones and the knife sweep

of mind on wood. Suddenly a cry announces
now. "Look," my younger sister screams, "come
quick!" And we tumble stammering through the door
across the brook to the yard's edge. Beyond

the fence a muted heron stands, frozen in blue
behind the stalks of winter grass. We watch
it seems forever, brothers and sisters waiting
for a sign. The heron does not move. You have spoken.

III.

We speak our peace. From the childhood jumble of letters
we build the blocks of our saying. We promise to be
better. We sew the thread of your wishes into
the cloth of time, then arc westward, southward

to our homes. Suns rise and set. Roads ice
and thaw and ice again. One night I telephone
your house. The caretaker answers. "The bird's
still there," she says. "It hasn't moved."

My mind shifts into fifth. I had known the legendary
stillness of herons, but not this. I have no words.
Then a whisper on the phone. "It's not alive,
it's made of wood," she says. "I thought you knew

and staged the scene to take me in." But no one
knew except you, Emily, who must have watched
with rare delight to see us wonder at this
worthless bird, this fraudulent figure in the field.

IV.

Your laughter remains, and the beady eyes of this
wooden bird which sits beside my desk staring
at the whiteness of my page. You always liked a joke
and if God would speak and say you're somewhere

kicking your heels on some unsightly cloud
I'd laugh too and kiss the possum on the wall
you painted the previous fall. But God's as silent
as this bird, as silent as midwinter grass.

Time turns the joke to acid in our guts.
We miss the lines of wisdom on your face
and the way your mind raced like Secretariat
whom you loved, leaping with graceful strides

the lies of the public place. Our lives lie
littered in the streets, discards from the
tarnished plates of our rusted days. Desire crawls
whining toward earth's last hole. Teach us

what stays. Teach us soul's gold and the high
cry of gulls over the cliffs of pain.
Parched mouths wait. Cover us once again
with the blue green mantle of your living rain.

THOUSAND PETALLED LOTUS

1.

We sit in the small cafe in the heat of noon
fans whirring like circling birds in the dark
above our heads. You tell me of your mother,

how you sat by her side, watched and listened
in her last days. I am a vulture. I feed on tales.
I am tempted to steal your story, to say "I"

for you, but your tears come, and the great
clarity of your fine mind behind the weeping.
I know that I cannot. I hear your words.

The telephone jars your ear. The doctor.
Your mother is dying. No heroics, states
her living will. "Put her on a respirator,"

you say, seeing the urgent shapes of words
to be spoken, a lifetime of missed moments
to be filled before the purple blossom blooms.

You pack, skirts and blouses in her favorite
hues, drive to her side and wait for her eyes
to open. The respirator clicks breaths.

2.

You hear the rasping in and out of air.
You watch her frail body, thin as a child's.
Your mother is beautiful, says the nurse.

The next day she wakens, smiles to your
smile. She had not thought to see your face
again. She had travelled the tunnel, the light

had beckoned, then dark had thrust her back
to pain once more. You tell stories. She listens.
You sleep, then wake to find a note in blue:

"I'm hungry," her letter says. "I want
a chicken sandwich." You laugh, and the tears
come with the taste of chicken in your mouth.

That night she pulls the tube, and chews
each bite slowly, like some prisoner reprieved
to eat another meal, see another dawn

through the thickening bars. She will not
put it back. She wants to talk, to make
the sounds of words with her own tongue.

She will whisper to you in her own voice
something to be valued like great-grandmother's
opal broach worn at the throat for generations.

3.

On the fourth day she seizes the oxygen
with what's left of her good right hand.
She holds it by her side and waits.

Her lungs convulse, pushing the neck veins
hard, hard against the skin. Her body heaves
for life. You try to put it back, but her grip

is firm as the eagle's. Her eyes look you down.
All day you watch by her side. That night you rise,
but her grip stays you, again and again.

In the morning she is dead. You watch the life
leave her body from the toes upward, you watch
the life depart from the seven cosmic centers.

The cold begins in the genitals, the seat
of earth, then abdomen and navel, next
the flying heart, seat of compassion.

Then throat and eyebrows and last of all
the thousand petaled lotus, the crown
chakra, seat of life itself, throne of gods.

You tell me this in the dark cafe with fans
whirring and I feel the life rise, return
to life itself and my tears come for you

and the wisdom of your hands as they touch
your mother's face for the last time and close
her eyes. You take the gold ring with purple

amethyst from the small finger of her right
hand. You place it on your own and go to call
the others. The rest is for the gods to know.

Anthony S. Abbott

About the Author

Anthony Abbott was born in San Francisco, received his A.B. from Princeton University in 1957 and his Ph.D from Harvard in 1962. Since 1964 he has taught English at Davidson College in North Carolina.

A published critic, poet, and theologian, Anthony Abbott has won numerous awards including the Thomas H. McDill Award and the Anne Newman Poetry Award. *A Small Thing Like A Breath* is his second book of poetry.

Anthony S. Abbott